WHERE HAS ALL THE CREDIT GONE?

ON THE REAL CAUSES
OF THE RECESSION,
BANKING AND CREDIT
CRISES 2007/2008

A conventional analysis of our current
crises and an unconventional cure

By Colin Richard Webb

PUBLISHER

First published 2008 by Colin Richard Webb.

This edition published by Colin Richard Webb

72 Wensley Road Leeds LS7 2LS United Kingdom.

WHERE HAS ALL THE CREDIT GONE?
ON THE REAL CAUSES OF THE RECESSION, BANKING AND CREDIT CRISES 2007/2008

A conventional analysis of our current crises

and an unconventional cure

Copyright © Colin Richard Webb 2008

All rights reserved. The moral rights of the author have been asserted.

This publication is in copyright. Subject only to statutory exception and to the relevant collective licensing agreements, no part of this publication may be reproduced, stored in a retrieval system, or transmitted in any form or by any means, electrical, mechanical, photocopying, recording or otherwise, without the prior permission of the copyright owner, Colin Richard Webb.

This publication contains the text of an analysis,

"On the Real Causes of the Recession, Banking and Credit Crises 2007/2008" produced in November 2008 by Colin Richard Webb, based on conventional economics alone, together with a complete copy of the unconventional economic ideas of the First Ideas Edition of

"The Economics of Money, Poverty and Wealth and What We Should Do About It" (ISBN 978-0-9558482-0-9)

Copyright © Colin Richard Webb 2008

All rights reserved. The moral rights of the author have been asserted.

This publication is in copyright. Subject only to statutory exception and to the relevant collective licensing agreements, no part of this publication may be reproduced, stored in a retrieval system, or transmitted in any form or by any means, electrical, mechanical, photocopying, recording or otherwise, without the prior permission of the copyright owner, Colin Richard Webb.

This copy is reproduced here with the permission of Colin Richard Webb as publisher and as author and is subject to the conditions of copyright noted in the original work and noted above.

This work has an ISBN: 978-0-9558482-1-6 (paperback)

*In hope of a better future
in which we can learn
from the world's mistakes
better than we have done*

WHERE HAS ALL THE CREDIT GONE?

ON THE REAL CAUSES OF THE RECESSION,

BANKING AND CREDIT CRISES 2007/2008

A conventional analysis of our current crises

and an unconventional cure

If you want to read the conventional analysis first, please start at page 71, then return to what follows for the unconventional cure.

CONTENTS,

Preface

1 The Economics of Money,
   Poverty and Wealth and
   What We Should Do About It
   Preface,   i-iv
   Contents,   v-viii
   Text,   1-70

2 On The Real Causes Of The Recession, Banking
   And Credit Crises 2007/2008,   71-97

3 Copy Email to Professor Sachs on the above book
   and an alternative, unconventional solution to the
   credit crunch, together with explanatory note   99-100

4 Copy Email to UN expanding on ideas implicit
   in the above book concerning the Quantity Theory
   of Money, together with explanatory notes   101-105

WHERE HAS ALL THE CREDIT GONE?

ON THE REAL CAUSES OF THE RECESSION,

BANKING AND CREDIT CRISES 2007/2008

A conventional analysis of our current crises

and an unconventional cure

PREFACE

The analysis was sent to all UK political parties represented in the UK Parliament on 28th November 2008 as a collection of personal views of the current crises by Colin Richard Webb, author of "The Economics of Money, Poverty and Wealth and What We Should Do About It".

I would like to note that in chapter 19 I claimed I was not party political, and I am not; I first wrote some of those words in correspondence in 2005 and when the book was first published in May 2008 the words were still true, however since then the UK political parties have been adopting different positions and some are clearly more in line with the position the book proposes than other stances some may have adopted. Obviously who knows where political parties will be on these issues as time moves on and they become more familiar with these economic ideas.

I have not changed my position, or political independence, or the text of the "First Ideas Edition", reproduced here in full.

It is well worthwhile reading John Maynard Keynes, "The General Theory of Employment, Interest and Money", particularly chapter 22, "Notes on the Trade Cycle", and chapter 11, "The Marginal Efficiency of Capital", even if I do not necessarily share all his conclusions. It is a poignant read for our current times, particularly when you remember he wrote these words, which could so closely describe our current circumstances and events, so long ago.

Colin Webb

Leeds

28th November 2008

If you want to read my conventional analysis first, please start at page 71, then return to what follows for the unconventional cure …

THE ECONOMICS OF MONEY, POVERTY AND WEALTH AND WHAT WE SHOULD DO ABOUT IT

Colin Richard Webb

Leeds, United Kingdom

PUBLISHER

First published 2008 by Colin Richard Webb.

This edition published by Colin Richard Webb

72 Wensley Road Leeds LS7 2LS United Kingdom.

This book is sold subject to the condition that it shall not, by way of trade or otherwise, be lent, resold, hired out or otherwise circulated without the publisher's prior consent in any form of binding or cover other than that in which it is published and without a similar condition including this condition being imposed on the subsequent purchaser.

The Economics of Money, Poverty and Wealth

and What We Should Do About It - First Ideas Edition

Copyright © Colin Richard Webb 2008.

All rights reserved. The moral rights of the author have been asserted.

This publication is in copyright. Subject only to statutory exception and to the relevant collective licensing agreements, no part of this publication may be reproduced, stored in a retrieval system, or transmitted in any form or by any means, electronic, mechanical, photocopying, recording or otherwise, without the prior permission of the copyright owner, Colin Richard Webb.

Based on a First Draft Edition, 16th March 2007,

Copyright © Colin Richard Webb 2007, and on correspondence,

Copyright © Colin Richard Webb 2005, 2006, 2007.

All rights reserved. The moral rights of the author have been asserted.

ISBN: 978-0-9558482-0-9 (paperback)

For the family and all the future generations

THE ECONOMICS OF MONEY, POVERTY AND WEALTH AND WHAT WE SHOULD DO ABOUT IT

	CONTENTS,	i -iv
	Preface – The Problem of Poverty Around the World - Towards Ideas for a Solution,	v - viii

ESSENTIAL ECONOMIC INSIGHTS/IDEAS TO IDENTIFY THE ISSUES TO SOLVE POVERTY

1	Effective Demand and Supply, or Lack of Them,	1
2	Destruction of Value by Consumers,	3
3	Sources of Money,	5
4	Money as a Medium with its Own Inherent Mathematics,	9
5	Money as a Misused Human Tool,	13
6	Poverty is Inevitable Unless We Change Our System of Economics to Correct for the Operation of Money,	17

A POSSIBLE METHOD OF SOLVING POVERTY

7	One Possible Attempt at a Solution to Poverty – The International Loan from the Future,	21
8	Moving the Place Where Value (and Wealth) is Destroyed Away from the Individual Consumer,	23
9	Who Will Meet the Cost of Solving the Problem of Poverty,	25
10	Creating Wealth from the Poorest Consumers,	27

SOME PRACTICAL DIFFICULTIES TO BE OVERCOME ON THE WAY TO SOLVING POVERTY

11	Ensuring the Perception of Fairness for All and the Need for Work to be Done,	29
12	Inflation - Demand and Supply for Goods and Services Must be Expanded in a Synchronised and Harmonious Manner,	33
13	The Dangers of Expanding Existing Businesses and the Supply Side Overtrading Collapses Must be Avoided,	39

THE ECONOMICS OF MONEY, POVERTY AND WEALTH AND WHAT WE SHOULD DO ABOUT IT

CONSIDERATIONS OF THE INTERACTION WITH EXISTING ECONOMIC THEORIES

14	On Issues of the Economics of Money,	41
15	Macroeconomic Modelling,	47

ALTERNATIVE SIMILAR ACTION BY A SINGLE COUNTRY FOR ITS OWN BENEFIT

16	International Action or Action by an Individual Country – Exchange Rate Issues,	53
17	Action by One Country to Borrow for Poverty Alleviation and Economic Growth by Increasing Effective Demand,	55

THE NEED FOR APPROPRIATE INTERVENTION

18	Why We Should Take Action to Stop Poverty Around the World,	59
19	Political Reassurance and the Role of Governments in Economics,	63
20	The Need to Improve our Capitalism,	65

A VERY IMPORTANT DANGER TO AVOID

| 21 | A Further Danger to Avoid, but a Solution to the Problem of Poverty Can Be Found, | 67 |

THE ECONOMICS OF MONEY, POVERTY AND WEALTH AND WHAT WE SHOULD DO ABOUT IT

PREFACE

THE PROBLEM OF POVERTY AROUND THE WORLD - TOWARDS IDEAS FOR A SOLUTION

I have had some insights into the economic roots of poverty.

I hope that if you are reading this it is because you really want to help solve this worldwide problem. I trust that you will be prepared to read, think about and try to understand these ideas.

At first, some may appear simple and obvious statements, but do not be deceived as they may be more subtle and more sophisticated than that. I attach over the following pages what I hope will convey the main thrust of the ideas I have realised.

Please persevere because the issues are so important. It is the combination of a few key ideas that is necessary to really get to understand the real power of the ideas I have had and put together.

If you just don't "get it", then please keep trying to reach an understanding of them. It is only by using the ideas together that you will realise, as I have begun to do to some extent, just how much they can allow us to change the world for the better.

I have tried to set out the minimum set of ideas I started from and which need to be thought about and combined together, as 31 numbered paragraphs, broken down into the first five chapters in small groups to try to make the ideas easier to assimilate. However one must combine these ideas to really appreciate the full scope of what is possible and that is clearly not an easy task, despite what may appear the simplicity of some of the individual concepts set out.

I suggest that when you reach the end of chapter five you ensure you read chapter six, but then you try to review all 31 numbered paragraphs set out in the first five chapters – I have kept these deliberately short and to the point without elaboration so that combining them into a mind may be possible. So I make no apology for the brevity of certain chapters, they are like this to aid the reader in gaining as easily as possible the understanding of the whole of the necessary combination of these ideas.

Initially I thought the main solution to the problem of poverty, which I am proposing, might require a huge level of international agreement in order to implement the idea because of exchange rate movement problems that might hinder its use. Fortunately I have realised this potential obstacle can be overcome and turned instead to advantage if the plan were implemented properly, even in just one country, to alleviate poverty and boost that country's economy.

Certain of the ideas could be dangerously disruptive if people do not understand that a better, non-disruptive way to implement and benefit from them is preferable and possible. So a degree of responsibility in using and spreading the ideas may be required. On balance now, it is my judgment, that it is better that the way to end poverty is understood and eventually achieved rather than we persist with it for so many in the world indefinitely and cling to the false hope of only trading out of poverty. There may be risks of some social disruption if some people become impatient with their lot, upon realising some of what these ideas imply, however, despite this, progress to solve poverty must be made.

It is my sincere wish that people will learn from what the world has suffered in the nineteenth century, twentieth century and the start of the twenty-first century and we may use our minds and knowledge to avoid conflict within and between societies as we try to move towards a better future and a better way of doing things in the world for everybody in a non-violent and peaceful way.

It is my hope that these ideas will be understood and, with enough peaceful pressure from the public, that politicians in this country and around the world will choose to show their humanity and act so that perhaps action to really end poverty around the world can start in my country, or perhaps in yours.

Colin Webb

Leeds

16th March 2007 – as amended 18th April 2008

ESSENTIAL ECONOMIC INSIGHTS/IDEAS TO IDENTIFY THE ISSUES TO SOLVE POVERTY

CHAPTER ONE

EFFECTIVE DEMAND AND SUPPLY, OR LACK OF THEM

1. **Supply and demand curves determining price and level of supply depend upon the effective demand*** - i.e. the level of demand backed by real buying power of money available to be spent to deliver that demand.

2. As a corollary, **lack of effective demand means that it is not possible to generate a supply to meet what may be a need of the individual who does not have effective demand** - i.e. the person who does not have the money to have effective demand will not be able to generate a supply to meet their needs and will therefore suffer unmet needs.

3. As a second corollary, **the scale of supply will be lower than otherwise possible because it will only match the effective demand.** Hence if money could be provided to convert people, who are with need but without the money to have any effective demand, into people with the money to exercise effective demand to meet their needs then a supply to meet their needs could happen in a way it would otherwise never do under current economic arrangements.

Further notes on Chapter One key points:-

Note that after a period of temporary inflation where demand may exceed supply, the higher level of supply to meet the greater demand may lead to lower overall prices for all supplied (due to suppliers' cost efficiencies on economies of scale). Overall total money generated for the supply businesses and economy may be increased as well, although that might require more total money to exist in the economy to sustain the greater activity level.

* Note the idea of effective demand I am using in this sense is nearer to Adam Smith's "effectual demand" involved in the pricing for any particular commodity, than John Maynard Keynes' aggregate effective demand for a whole economy, albeit that may, or may not, be the sum of all particular effective demands for all markets within an economy. I am considering what effective demand means for those particular individuals in the economy involved in the market, who actually can or cannot participate in the transactions which comprise that particular market. One could say that by its conventional definition effective demand is that demand which results from the market price and is that of those who participate in the market, but that way of looking at the concept means that it would not be possible to consider how it could be changed or improved and what it means for those without such demand who are simply ignored on this basis. Perhaps that is one reason these issues have not been examined thoroughly enough hitherto.

ESSENTIAL ECONOMIC INSIGHTS/IDEAS TO IDENTIFY THE ISSUES TO SOLVE POVERTY

CHAPTER TWO

DESTRUCTION OF VALUE BY CONSUMERS

4. **Consumers destroy value when they consume - i.e. they part with money to obtain what they will consume and so will lose money/part with money and then the act of consuming will destroy the consumable so that its value is lost** (or in some instances perhaps only reduced).

5. As a corollary, unless consumers can replace their money (through earning or otherwise) they will reduce their monetary wealth by exchanging money for consumables and consuming them until they run out of money and can no longer consume.

6. As a second corollary, unless a person has a source of income or replacement money, their acts of consuming will tend to reduce their money, as it is exchanged for consumables, until they reach a state of lack of effective demand (i.e. not enough money).

7. As a third corollary, people who start with no money, will not have any effective demand to create a supply to meet their needs and will be unable to obtain consumables to consume, unless a means can be found to let them have money, through trade, work, benefits, or aid.

ESSENTIAL ECONOMIC INSIGHTS/IDEAS TO IDENTIFY THE ISSUES TO SOLVE POVERTY

CHAPTER THREE

SOURCES OF MONEY

8. In order to obtain money, apart from benefits or aid, one must find something to trade for money, or work (trade one's labour or time), or one could say, beg, borrow or steal. Obviously, the latter is unacceptable.

9. As a corollary, in order to trade one must obtain something to trade and this may mean that if one does not have some money to acquire a stock of goods to trade one may not be able to start a system of trading exchange to generate profit and money as an income stream.

10. Hence, borrowing to get started may be needed and provision of finance to allow the poorest (or indeed anyone) to start up businesses is therefore important.

11. As a second corollary, without the options to trade, or work, or without goods/assets to sell, people will not be able to obtain money to buy consumables and live unless an alternative way to provide them with money is found. This is a rationale for aid and benefit provision.

12. Following on from that, this support may be increasingly important as we find ways to produce with machines and robots and have less need for workforces of people in the production processes and economies.

13. A further issue will be that the domination of trade and provision by larger organisations, increasingly on a global basis, may undermine opportunities for individuals and smaller organisations to engage in trade, illustrated perhaps by a trend away from small shops to supermarkets and high street chains.

14. In our current progression, diminishing trading opportunities for some and work opportunities for others may eliminate their essential sources of income needed for self sufficiency in our interconnected interdependent economic lives.

15. I will highlight an important theme of Adam Smith that could be paraphrased as "no man is an island"* in economic terms. We all depend on others' efforts to some extent for what we need. This gives the lie to an exclusively selfish approach to life, even if Adam Smith also highlighted a natural human tendency to look after one's own interest first. Of course everyone is concerned about their own means of earning or getting a living for themselves and their families. Yes, that motivates people to economic behaviour to get their money, but real people are much more than just the work they do for that reason.

*"No man is an island" is a quote from John Donne's Meditation XVII.

ESSENTIAL ECONOMIC INSIGHTS/IDEAS TO IDENTIFY THE ISSUES TO SOLVE POVERTY

CHAPTER FOUR

MONEY AS A MEDIUM WITH ITS OWN INHERENT MATHEMATICS

16. **Money is the medium of exchange, but the mathematics of money is based on a simple additive and subtractive model - I give you money for what I want to buy and you give me the goods/services and receive the money.**

17. Hence, **it is not possible to buy with money without passing monetary wealth from the buyer to the seller - just because the mathematical model of money is inevitably taking from one person and giving to the other party to the transaction.**

18. As a corollary, wealth flows with money to the producers and suppliers of consumables and hence any who receive from that, e.g. governments in sales and other taxes, workers in the supply and provision businesses, suppliers for raw material and other supplies in the supply chain, through rents for properties in use, through interest for

finance in use and through profits and dividends to owners and shareholders of such businesses, companies and enterprises etc.

19. As a second corollary reduction of wealth occurs for the purchasers in any transaction and returning to the issue of consumers consuming consumables and destroying the value of what they have consumed, it follows that the mathematics of money means that the operation of a money transaction alone drives down the wealth of an individual purchaser.

20. **Hence the operation of money transactions alone will reduce one individual's wealth and tend towards moving any purchaser towards poverty, whilst equally increasing someone else's wealth.**

21. As a corollary, it really is the case that a rich person's wealth represents other people's poverty - this is not to blame - **it is merely to note the economic truth that each money transaction has someone who gains money and someone who parts with it.**

N. B. It may be argued where someone spends to acquire something to sell on (perhaps as stock or an investment) that the purchaser's wealth is not necessarily diminished by the act of purchase (they may even have the better of the deal), but in fact their monetary wealth has been reduced and is only restored, for better or worse, when the item is sold.

In other words, it is the act of selling the item that brings them (or restores to them, or enhances) their monetary wealth.

22. Hence, **it is therefore impossible to gain money without someone else having parted with it; that is the inherent mathematics of our current economics, which was created, perhaps thoughtlessly, by ancient man and we still apply today, because no one has realised we need not suffer this anymore.**

23. I note that it may be perfectly appropriate for someone to gain profit and wealth, when others have parted with their money to get and receive what they wanted - there is nothing wrong in that - it is what an economic system should do, i.e. provide what people want and reward those that provide it, so they will do so.

24. However **what we can do without is the suffering of the downside punishment of the operation of money. The mathematical operation of money often inflicts the suffering on some through no fault of their own, or excludes others altogether from the possibility of gain, sometimes through accident or consequence of history and personal circumstance.**

ESSENTIAL ECONOMIC INSIGHTS/IDEAS TO IDENTIFY THE ISSUES TO SOLVE POVERTY

CHAPTER FIVE

MONEY AS A MISUSED HUMAN TOOL

25. **Money is a tool for allowing exchange of fair value - but it is flawed in its operation because the economic systems it generates create consumers who destroy value, and create some who end without any money and are unable to consume, who must reside in poverty just because of the inexorable operation of the mathematics of money, and the fact that the current economic systems based on it tend to ignore those without money and buying power, or those with nothing, so preventing them joining the economic success and preventing them from enjoying economic participation.**

26. The divisions in society from richest to poorest and the defining characteristics of their relations are all generated out of this simple aspect of each transaction with money; for every transaction there is someone who gains money and someone who parts with it. For those who cannot gain more money than they part with, poverty is inevitable.

27. **This bleak truth is the reality that poverty will remain with all our societies until we modify our economics to correct for the dreadful downside half of the operation of money and the destruction of value by consuming that takes place with every individual consumer.**

28. As a corollary, trade alone will not solve the problem of poverty, which is not to say that trade is not necessarily worthwhile for individuals or nations, and is not to say that it will not create wealth for some, but it is to note that it will equally (in monetary extent) drive many others to at least a reduction in their monetary wealth, and so some into poverty.

29. As a second corollary, trickle down of wealth is also misconceived as the wealth has to be generated initially and can only be accumulated by creation of the equal and opposite downside of each transaction of money, i.e. the others who have all parted with their money in creating the wealth of the wealthy. Trickle down is only partially reversing that. Of course, trickle down is a real phenomena and to the extent it is reversing the previous wealth created, or increasing overall economic activity levels, it is welcome, of course, but it will never be the complete cure for our economic ills.

30. Money is a human tool, but our lack of understanding about its operation means that for thousands of years, human beings have been being determined and shaped by the tool and what it does to us all in our lives rather than allowing us to solve our problems and difficulties and improve all our situations.

31. As a conclusion, we must take back control over the tool of money in order to prevent its tendency to separate us into different groups, to cause a tendency in some towards criminality, to cause conflicts over resources and to cause a propensity to lead to empire building, greed and wars for resources etc.

ESSENTIAL ECONOMIC INSIGHTS/IDEAS TO IDENTIFY THE ISSUES TO SOLVE POVERTY

CHAPTER SIX

POVERTY IS INEVITABLE UNLESS WE CHANGE OUR SYSTEM OF ECONOMICS TO CORRECT FOR THE OPERATION OF MONEY

You may get the impression from what I have written that I am saying poverty cannot be avoided, but that is the opposite of what I am really saying; I am saying that we cannot and will not solve the issue of poverty until we recognise what the problem really is, and that is the problem of the operation of money, the mathematics of money, the effect of consumption destroying value and the lack of effective demand of the poor so created.

When we understand the problem and how it afflicts the whole world, and always will under current economic arrangements, then we can tackle the problem and design a solution to allow all to join in full economic participation, so all can have effective demand to produce a supply to meet at least their needs and wants.

I am not sure whether the preceding ideas cover all the essential points of describing the problem of poverty and how it arises and persists, but as you can see the interplay of all these ideas is a complicated matter, which at least describes a substantial part of the problem, to enable a start towards finding a solution to be attempted.

No doubt in the reader's experience of encountering poverty's effects you may think I have omitted some aspects and perhaps you will think it is too Western in considering consumers, when the world's poorest, no doubt, start and stay with nothing and never get to consume. However that is part of my point, we must change that to allow them to become consumers and obtain effective demand. When we do that we will generate new customers for all of the world's businesses; more turnover, more profit, more tax revenues, more activity and much more economic growth to the benefit of rich and poor. We must repeat feeding money into the poorest so that as they consume they can continue to do so despite having used what they are given to start with.

We, perhaps, need to do more than just pump money into the poorest, otherwise we might only generate inflation to take away the real benefit of the actions. We will need to pump money into infrastructure and supply and provision at the same time so that supply to meet the increased effective demand can be expanded to match it and avoid some of the inflationary pressure.

A cynic might try to characterise and dismiss what I have said by saying it is no more than saying poor people have no money, big deal, big surprise, but that would be to ignore the key reasons why we should do something about this that I have outlined; that lack of effective demand of the poor restricts the total economic activity that could be achieved (and so, for instance, some businesses will currently close and shut down when perhaps with more custom they need not) and that **money is our tool, which we deny to many, so as a species we need to do better with our tools. We need to use our money and our brains better to achieve a better mathematics of money and economic systems.**

You might say that the latter point only amounts to an appeal to people's humanity and others have tried all that, and that the effective demand arguments have been tried by John Maynard Keynes already, but in reality I am providing the logical and mathematical arguments to expose the lack of humanity of those who will not take action to help our fellow humans - they can no longer hide behind economic and lack of resources arguments, which no doubt you will have heard so many times already.

More importantly there is now a case that not taking any action to solve the plight of the poor is holding all humanity's progress back from what could be achieved.

My breakthrough really is to highlight how the creation of rich and poor stems out of the operation of monetary transactions as a result of the mathematics, in each and every transaction, of money alone.

Our ancestors, in ignorance, chose to use the tool of money and its mathematics, so we can choose to change it, now that we can see it produces so much hardship and so large a set of difficulties and hindrance to progress for humanity.

A POSSIBLE METHOD OF SOLVING POVERTY

CHAPTER SEVEN

ONE POSSIBLE ATTEMPT AT A SOLUTION TO POVERTY - THE INTERNATIONAL LOAN FROM THE FUTURE

Having attempted an analysis of some aspects of the problem of poverty - what about a solution?

Several methods are possible to attempt to alter the mathematics of money. The one which I have produced, and like because it is simple and elegant and could be used and implemented very quickly, involves a concept of an international loan from the future.

The idea is based on adding constants to each side of an equation; add a loan and a matching amount of money to use (in perhaps the IMF or World Bank or a subsidiary's books), **keep the loan outstanding as a constant, use the money to develop the world - give out to the poorest to give them effective demand and to the industries and agriculture involved in supplying their demand** - the increase in world growth achieved will grow the world economy and the loan remains as a constant into the future.

You can view the loan as having been added to the current level of debt but also to the future level of debt and retained as a constant in the equations - no more than a book liability of countries receiving the benefit of the loan to their (new and existing) consumers and suppliers, **which can be retained indefinitely as a constant,** or repaid later when it will seem paltry compared to the future level of the world's economy, or indeed even written off because of the following aspect.

A POSSIBLE METHOD OF SOLVING POVERTY

CHAPTER EIGHT
MOVING THE PLACE WHERE VALUE (AND WEALTH) IS DESTROYED AWAY FROM THE INDIVIDUAL CONSUMER

The real point of the idea of the international loan from the future is to enable money to be given out to all consumers and the real idea is to move the place of destruction of value away from the consumer.

We can't actually move the destruction inherent in the act of consumption, but we can move the monetary financial loss away from the individual.

This is by giving them money to meet their consumption, i.e., to replace their money that they have spent on items to be consumed.

By centralising the value of consumption by paying the consumers money obtained from a world loan "from the future", we can make the point of destruction of monetary value a centralised institution, e.g. perhaps the IMF or World Bank, or a subsidiary, and write off the loan in that institution's books, or just keep it outstanding indefinitely.

In effect it just allows the world to overcome the problem of money's bad half by moving it from where it bites upon individual lives to a central world place where the effects of "the loss of money spent on consumption" may be pretty innocuous, instead of the devastating problem it currently is.

A POSSIBLE METHOD OF SOLVING POVERTY

CHAPTER NINE

WHO WILL MEET THE COST OF SOLVING THE PROBLEM OF POVERTY

All the money put into the world's economy from the international loan "from the future" will produce someone's increased monetary wealth and so the debt, if it ever needed to be repaid, could have repayments sourced out of the world's taxes on the wealthy who will have gained from it in the long run.

There is a good case for saying those who gain most from the operation of money and its economic systems should be happy to meet these costs out of taxation in any event.

However note that the loan allows them to postpone meeting this cost of money to the poorest and supply provision directly. For the rich it is an opportunity to gain from the bigger economy and a postponement of the time to pay for it through taxes, so on this basis the loan is in the interest of the rich as well as the poor.

However even better than this, is the fact that strictly on the arguments I am putting forward loan repayment is not really necessary (or appropriate, in my view) as a loan write off would merely be representing the destruction of value happening with consumers consuming; we will have just displaced that to a harmless place.

Whether we write the loan off or keep it outstanding indefinitely really will not matter, as long as we keep repeating the loan to maintain a flow of funds into the poor and to consumers and to the supply side of the world's economy to grow its monetary wealth, but, more importantly of course, grow its level of activity and its new successes in meeting what everyone needs and wants.

Note that the mathematics of the solution I am proposing involves adding a constant on both sides of the equations. On one side it can be a total, perhaps, for example, 6,000,000,000 little constants equal to one big constant. On this mathematical basis of adding a constant to each side of an equation, one could add any number of constants to both sides of the equation, each of any size one wanted and one could add constants to the equations as many times as one wanted or needed to do and the mathematics will make it work. Mathematics can be so beautiful.

A POSSIBLE METHOD OF SOLVING POVERTY

CHAPTER TEN

CREATING WEALTH FROM THE POOREST CONSUMERS

The effect of this international loan "from the future" plan is to transform the lives and life chances of the poorest around the world, in every society, by allowing them money to create an effective demand for goods and services they need and want.

It will trickle up to benefit every level of the current economic system to increase the wealth and employment chances of every citizen in every country and particularly will flow up to even the richest.

This plan really has the potential to be a win/win for everyone.

SOME PRACTICAL DIFFICULTIES TO BE OVERCOME ON THE WAY TO SOLVING POVERTY

CHAPTER ELEVEN
ENSURING THE PERCEPTION OF FAIRNESS FOR ALL AND THE NEED FOR WORK TO BE DONE

One difficulty is the balance needed between aid to the poorest, with support to industries supplying the extra supply to their extra demand, and retaining some need for other people to continue to work in their existing jobs and roles and receive some incentive from monetary rewards to allow that to continue unabated and stability to be retained.

The answer in the short run may be in the way in which on this plan money is given to all consumers, not least to overcome fairness issues the mid-tiers of societies may raise if they did not receive when others who are not working receive apparently for no reason, other than that most important reason - to get them to spend.

Will people complain if they are also benefiting?

The question of how much of a consumer's money needs to be provided is a vital issue.

In principle, it could all be provided, but then why would people do the work that needs to be done? From the goodness of their hearts? As not everyone will believe that could happen, it therefore becomes a matter of social policy to strike the balance between money provision for all consumers' needs and wants, and the extent to which they must seek to work or trade to obtain their money to spend on what they desire, so that all the work, that needs to be done to meet everyone's needs and wants, can happen.

Achieving a smooth transition may present challenges, but we must transition to money provision for those that need it and creation of the supply for everyone's needs and wants.

In the long run, we may see the effect of the plan could be to allow people to choose to work, and employment in some activity available for all who wish to, without the current constraints of finance limiting the employments available and creating unwanted unemployment and suffering from that, on so great a scale as we see in the world, at the moment.

It may be that although considerable economic growth and opportunities for work around the world can be created using these mechanisms and ideas, it may actually free the amount of time workers need to work. So each can spend and devote less time to work and can achieve a better work/life balance, with more time available for the great boon of family life. This may also be the case as we increasingly use robots to replace the labour of men and women.

Part-time working hours may become the norm, as we make progress in the future.

However as there will be less need for a workforce in the future we must realise that we must find alternative ways of providing the money, that people need to survive and to consume, to them.

SOME PRACTICAL DIFFICULTIES TO BE OVERCOME ON THE WAY TO SOLVING POVERTY

CHAPTER TWELVE

INFLATION - DEMAND AND SUPPLY FOR GOODS AND SERVICES MUST BE EXPANDED IN A SYNCHRONISED AND HARMONIOUS MANNER

Another issue is the management of inflationary pressures which will be important as economies can expand very, very quickly using this international loan "from the future" mechanism.

Milton Friedman flags up the impact of money supply leading to inflation, but this is not the whole story.

There is inflation when there is extra demand, or money supplied to allow this, without increasing a supply to match the demand at the same time.

Keynes multiplier expansion of the economy works by expanding some supply side/infrastructure provision whilst injecting money into the economy through this, and so will lead to some economic growth, but also inflation as it injects money to allow some employed on the projects to have money and increase their demand in the economy, but without injection into the rest of the supply side to meet their extra demand for goods and services there will also be inflationary pressure.

So provision of finance facilities to allow existing businesses and supply to expand to match the injection of extra demand is also needed.

The inflation when demand is increased may be only a natural, temporary phenomenon until supply rises. The increased price could be viewed as part of the process that attracts extra suppliers into the (to be enlarged) market, until the extra supply brings the pricing down. Not all inflation is a bad thing; sometimes it is a necessary part of market adjustments operating properly and efficiently, when new supply (perhaps in the form of other competitors) is needed in a market.

On this basis it could be said that help to aid supply provision is only damping down the price increases and the adverse effects of inflation to those other existing consumers in the market and may limit the price attracting new suppliers to the market. However damped down by extra help to supply provision, even the pre-existing price may be enough to create the extra supply needed, from new or existing suppliers to the market, because the supply to the extra numbers of consumers is still producing more money and profit for the suppliers.

Hence I believe limited, temporary, active support, or intervention, to limit transitional inflation by assisting supply provision expansion would be desirable.

It is very important to ensure that action to expand food supply production and availability is taken and more food is available to the market in a timely manner, or the extra cash to the poorest competing for the same food levels may lead to higher prices and lack of availability and starvation issues; a King Midas problem, lots of money for the food, but not enough food to eat.

Given the inherent time delay between starting to increase crop levels and food production output it may be necessary to plan the expansion of agriculture to ensure enough food supplies are available to a country's or the world's markets when the cash is injected to the poorest and economy.

In a wider context for all countries in the world, adopting the plan or not, the same point re food supplies is clearly important. Ensuring security of food supplies for all is a vital task for the world economy which we seem to have lost sight of recently. In the 1960's when there were in the region of 3 billion people on the planet, the huge task of increasing food production for the expected "population explosion" was understood to be one of the major challenges for humanity.

On the whole, until recently, the world met that challenge of increased agricultural food production. This may have been jeopardized by the switch of farm land to bio-fuel crops and seeking just more money and profit instead of agricultural production for food. The switch reduces levels of food supply and creates some of the large inflation of food prices and shortages recently seen.

Now with about 6 billion people we face a forecast ahead of a rising population that might reach, we are told, 9 billion in the next 40 to 50 years, and there may be many more than that. We have proved in the last 40 years that we can meet the agricultural production expansion needed to raise enough food to feed an extra 3 billion, if we apply our efforts to the tasks to increase productive agricultural land in use for food production and its yields.

However we need to realise the need to maintain the success of the last generations and progress its expansion of agricultural food production to deliver the necessary additional food supplies to feed all of the world's population fully, despite any setbacks which might arise from changing climate patterns etc.

I note none of this requires any genetic modification to our foods – we have all the plants and animals we need – we just need to expand their numbers, use more land for these purposes and distribute food to all.

So we will need to support and encourage agricultural production for a level of increase of production much more than the obvious 50% uplift needed.

With a solution to poverty, will come a need to increase food production to levels appropriate to feed fully all the world population, whereas at the moment too many in the world must scrape by without a full diet.

The additional meat production needed clearly also requires the appropriate additional animal feed supplies to be produced, etc.

However, it can all be done if enough of us apply our minds, work and efforts to these important tasks of keeping us all well fed and healthy. More importantly, it must be done.

SOME PRACTICAL DIFFICULTIES TO BE OVERCOME ON THE WAY TO SOLVING POVERTY

CHAPTER THIRTEEN

THE DANGERS OF EXPANDING EXISTING BUSINESSES AND THE SUPPLY SIDE OVERTRADING COLLAPSES MUST BE AVOIDED

A further danger is that the rapid expansion of ordinary businesses can be dangerous and risk overtrading collapses from lack of available finance when companies expand their profitable activities to supply new demands too quickly.

The additional activity of itself can denude the business of cash and finance resources it needs as it pays creditors for the increased levels of goods taken into stock and sold onto its extra customers and this ties the company's available finances into increased levels of stock and debtors that may just be appropriate to the new higher level of activity, but which need to be financed. There can be quite a time lag before the extra profit, arising from the extra sales, flows in to provide enough new finance to sustain those activity levels and levels of stock and debtors.

This cash flow deficiency can kill normal profitable businesses if finance is not available to see them through the transition.

This danger, which can be avoided by steady rates of growth by individual trading companies and organisations, can also be overcome by provision of the necessary temporary finance to overcome the difficulty the businesses which need to expand rapidly may face.

This could actually give governments a mechanism for putting funding into expanding supply side businesses out of the international loan "from the future", as long as everyone realises the need to seek such help and for governments to provide such help in a timely fashion to sustain the additional activity levels until the finance arising out of profits from the extra sales activity arrives to replace the temporary loans needed to sustain the businesses in the meantime.

CONSIDERATIONS OF THE INTERACTION WITH EXISTING ECONOMIC THEORIES

CHAPTER FOURTEEN

ON ISSUES OF THE ECONOMICS OF MONEY

One point here is that sometimes even healthy companies can find that they are short of finance and just do not have enough money to do all the things they would like and could do, just like individuals.

Lack of money limits a great many people from doing what they can and would like to be able to do.

This is not about the coinage or circulating money in the world as Adam Smith characterised money - it is about the reality that every transaction involving money has a monetary value and a monetary impact on both purchaser and seller, in terms of their monetary wealth. The really key aspect of money is the mathematical effect of money in every transaction for all sellers and all purchasers, and the sum of all their monetary wealth, which statement is not to diminish the importance of the economic impact of non monetary wealth or value.

The economics and thinking of Adam Smith about value has obscured and deflected attention away from these important aspects of the effect of money, to which we have perhaps only realised to pay a little more attention, at least to a small extent, with Milton Friedman's attention on the money supply. Hopefully having realised the importance of money, in each money transaction and in the total of money transactions, I have now flagged up the need to address these issues of how poverty is currently created and economic activity restricted and how we can start to change things for the better.

Adam Smith had particular reasons for arguing for the "cheap" paper money to use in circulation in the economy in contrast to the previous ages' obsessions with gold and silver (coinage etc) and to encourage countries to move away from being dominated by such considerations, which in his view at the time, was inhibiting the development of trade due to other people's arguments in favour of having regard to the gold and silver held by a country, and restricting its use in buying goods etc. from overseas.

These considerations, in my view, propelled him into arguing for the insignificance of the value of the actual money required to be used for a transaction, in contrast to, in Adam Smith's view, the real value of the other half of the transaction.

Adam Smith argues that the value is not both the non-monetary item in a transaction and the value of the money used in the transaction (albeit they are equal) and so chooses to select the value of the non-monetary item. He chooses therefore to dismiss the value of the monetary side of the transaction (and in the process consideration of its effects) by excluding it in the way he sets out when discussing circulating money. He prefers to dwell on the circulation of money rather than money's real functional impact at the point of the transaction upon the monetary position of purchaser and seller.

However one could just as easily take the opposite stance because the value of the non-monetary item and the money involved in the transaction are equal.

In fact Adam Smith is here a little self contradictory in that in describing the nominal money value of a transaction as the actual money value of the transaction in a given time and place he states, very clearly in Book I chapter 5 of An Enquiry into the Nature and Causes of the Wealth of Nations, that,

"But though in establishing perpetual rents, or even in letting very long leases, it may be of use to distinguish between real and nominal price; it is of none in buying and selling, the more common and ordinary transactions of human life." (Book I. chapter 5.18)

"At the same time and place the real and the nominal price of all commodities are exactly in proportion to one another. The more or less money you get for any commodity, in the London market, for example, the more or less labour it will at that time and place enable you to purchase or command. At the same time and place, therefore, money is the exact measure of the real exchangeable value of all commodities. It is so, however, at the same time and place only." (Book I. chapter 5.19)

(Book I. chapter 5.20 omitted)

"As it is the nominal or money price of goods, therefore, which finally determines the prudence or imprudence of all purchases and sales, and thereby regulates almost the whole business of common life in which price is concerned, we cannot wonder that it should have been so much more attended to than the real price."

(Book I. chapter 5.21)

Thereby, Adam Smith, despite proceeding in other places in his work, at least twice (and with much emphasis), to reject the use of the nominal value of money as the appropriate measure of a transaction or as the object of investigation as to wealth, a prejudice which he creates and which lingers in economic circles to this day, actually Adam Smith, in fact, gives us a sound foundation as to why the effect of each and every transaction can be measured by that nominal price, or of course, equal actual monetary level of the transaction.

This is because every transaction occurs in a time and place and so that at that time in that place that nominal price and price actually paid is a correct measure of the transaction, but also, and this is the more hidden point, of its functional, and real, impact on the monetary position of both purchaser and seller and so of their respective monetary wealth. As a corollary it is appropriate, to consider every transaction in terms of its monetary value and to consider its effect or monetary consequence on every purchaser and seller and upon their monetary wealth.

Adam Smith, for whatever motives, was keen to move people's thoughts away from seeking monetary wealth for its own sake, and I entirely agree with his notion that money held by a person is valuable to them only to the extent of what it can obtain for the person. Money so held is really just waiting to be used and to some extent does not fulfil its function for the individual until it is spent - i.e. accumulating more money for one's self than one will ever use in one's lifetime represents a little bit of a waste of a person's time, if they are truly only selfish, as Adam Smith's basis for economics would have us believe all to be, when operating in the economy.

However I will note that it is my conviction that our species has done well because we co-operate with each other and that it is those that do so for mutual benefit of the species that will achieve most for it.

That would be my rationale as to why people who are good at creating activity in the economy and profiting from their endeavour should continue to spend their time doing what they are good at, albeit they could look to put their resulting wealth to better use for others in the species, or for the species as a whole, rather than just storing up surplus and unnecessary super wealth way beyond what they will ever personally need to use. To some extent our systems of investment allow wealth invested to be put into use in the economies of our societies, so perhaps this is academic economically.

I trust I have outlined what must be considered about money and its operation in each transaction, and why it is appropriate to do so, despite some conventional economic wisdom, arising out of Adam Smith's apparent inconsistency on the issue of money. As I have attempted to note there may have been pressing issues or other reasons in his day that may have led him to this inconsistency. In my view this does not diminish some of the other enormous achievements Adam Smith realised in his great work.

CONSIDERATIONS OF THE INTERACTION WITH EXISTING ECONOMIC THEORIES

CHAPTER FIFTEEN

MACROECONOMIC MODELLING

John Maynard Keynes, in developing, and in the view of some, founding, a macroeconomic approach based on an aggregate effective demand model, failed to underpin the approach to aggregating the total effect of transactions and of individual and organisational monetary wealth, because he failed to correct Adam Smith and his classical economics' approach to money and instead followed them to dwell on the actual money in circulation, and how its price (in interest) is determined as if it were a commodity.

A partial correction has been forced upon economics as people attempted to model economics with computer and mathematical modelling of whole economies, such as circular flow models, but these have still to some extent been forced into following Adam Smith based current conventional wisdom and concentration upon the circulation of money (as set out by Adam Smith's framework of analysis), rather than the sum of individual, corporate, and organisational monetary wealth and how that is changing and interacting at the transaction level, which is the real economy. Some corrections to the classical models have been achieved however with some corrections for "wealth effects" in some economic considerations, and sometimes the real functional impacts of money in transactions have been considered.

However in recent decades debate raged (and, at the time of writing, may still rage) about whether macroeconomic analysis has any merit at all and whether it is appropriate or not.

The truth is an aggregation of transactions and the impact on individuals and organisations would be appropriate, if it were being done on a full and appropriate basis to consider the functional monetary wealth and the flows of monetary wealth as well as the non-monetary flows arising from each and every transaction.

Of course, the human behaviour of individuals and groups in different circumstances, and markets etc., is an essential aspect of any economics in which human beings are actively involved.

Oh what imperfect, irrational, uncontrolled, and free creatures we can be.

The schism between actual money in circulation and the functional effect of money that was an emerging issue in the time leading up to Adam Smith's analysis, and as it has persisted in some debates about returning to the gold standard etc ever since, is a real schism and means that we must model two flows of money:-

1. Its functional flow and effect on the wealth of both parties to a transaction. It is the interaction between holders of that wealth (whether that be in monetary form or non-monetary form - ready for sale) that really drives the transactions (or more accurately the monetary wealth aspects are at least half the drive behind any particular transaction with the non-monetary half being the other driving force behind a transaction.)

2. Its operation as a physical commodity - i.e. an item in circulation. Note here that this circulation does not necessarily mean a physical unit like a coin or a paper note, although in some economic circumstances it might.

The monetarists have struggled to define money in circulation for some time and this is their problem - in that demand for money, as well as being in part the demand for or supply of the physical money governments inject into economies to have as money in circulation, is connected to its functional use in transactions, and more specifically, its requirement by and availability to individuals and companies and organisations within their available financing to allow them to undertake the transactions they wish to do.

We may have to model two sets of flows of money, albeit modelling the monetary wealth flows between the monetary wealth of individuals and organisations etc, as well as the specifically circulating money, may do this.

In other words we should look to both sides, and the sum of the monetary and non-monetary effects (as separate flows), of each and every transaction across all transactions, but also across all parties to the transactions in an economy, if we want to successfully see how it works.

Of course, if we adopt an approach of including the wealth of all individuals in examining the sum of the economy of a society, one might raise issues of whether the wealth is that of the individuals or that of the society. It is important to reassure people that when one summates across an economy that one is not seeking to claim ownership over their wealth.

Marx and others may have fallen into the mistake of presuming the state's rights and "ownership" of all assets in a state, merely by considering a summation of all assets across a state or economy, which erroneously disregards and rides roughshod over the concepts of individual ownership of assets or of individual wealth.

The foundations of law and order and interactions in society have often been founded on individual ownership in order to resolve conflicts between individuals over disputed possessions or money. The presumption of state ownership overarching individual ownership has been a mistake bound to lead to conflict between individuals, and even collectives of individuals, and the state, except to the extent of agreed taxation for state provided services or activities.

Ownership over wealth issues might arise and be resisted by some, of course. However, generally, governments presume that they are entitled to tax the income and wealth of individuals and organisations within their nation's scope as they see fit anyway. So that now we have moved on from the age of kings that Adam Smith had to deal with perhaps this ought to be a non-issue; everyone can keep what they own, subject to meeting their fiscal responsibilities to the state.

However we will need to see the world move beyond the old thinking of Marx and Mao and Capitalist reactions to them, and more modern reactions to these, before we reach the position where it really is a non-issue.

Perhaps it makes it a little easier to understand why Adam Smith adopted the approach he did in his age, and why John Maynard Keynes in an age of post Communist revolution and clashing Fascism did not address the issue. Of course perhaps they just missed aspects of how money really works and how we should set about economics.

In the inevitable flux in price of every commodity and of money itself Adam Smith was correct to flag up the difficulty of measurement, when actual and nominal price and monetary exactitude is only possible in the time and place of every transaction.

One may say aggregations may be meaningless for this reason, but as no other basis for accounting has as much validity it may be a case of using the best, or least bad basis, of accurate economic measurement available to us.

This is after all what we require companies and others to do when accounting for their transactions on an historic cost basis with their annual or periodic accounts.

I believe other accounting bases of valuation proposed are often less accurate and have less validity than the historic cost basis, but that is clearly a matter of merely accounting and for what purpose one is accounting for and recording the transactions and the sum of transactions. The basis for appropriate accounting for taxation determination may be different from the basis appropriate for commercial decisions, or for investment decisions, or indeed for a country's economic data, although the more one uses different bases the more complex and more costly and error prone the process of accounting becomes.

ALTERNATIVE SIMILAR ACTION BY A SINGLE COUNTRY FOR ITS OWN BENEFIT

CHAPTER SIXTEEN

INTERNATIONAL ACTION OR ACTION BY AN INDIVIDUAL COUNTRY - EXCHANGE RATE ISSUES

I have tried to outline a specific practical plan as well as its economic and theoretical foundations.

Quantum leaps in activity levels could be possible with this mechanism of an international loan "from the future" to inject money to all consumers and the supply economy, if some of the issues can be ironed out, by experts, no doubt, more knowledgeable than I am.

I have outlined a possible international solution above - we can solve poverty, but we must gain the understanding of what the problem is before we can do so fully.

Now I will set out a single country version, because it may have to start somewhere before everyone wants to join in.

The international loan idea made me think initially we would need to get every country to sign up to the plan before it could be implemented and that was partly based on thinking that if one country borrowed on its own to use money to boost the spending power of its poor, that this would adversely affect the country's exchange rate (as it would on conventional wisdom).

However then I realised that if the action to borrow to increase a country's effective demand from its population acted as a boost to its economy then the exchange markets might back that country instead of penalise it as conventional wisdom might dictate at the moment. Particularly true, if the markets grew to understand the logic of why it would be good for a country's economy.

ALTERNATIVE SIMILAR ACTION BY A SINGLE COUNTRY FOR ITS OWN BENEFIT

CHAPTER SEVENTEEN
ACTION BY ONE COUNTRY TO BORROW FOR POVERTY ALLEVIATION AND ECONOMIC GROWTH BY INCREASING EFFECTIVE DEMAND

So in fact it would be possible for any one country to borrow to obtain money to give to its poorest, to its consumers, to its agriculture and the industries needed to expand supply to meet the consumers' extra effective demand. Supply expansion overall, and with distribution for an expanded supply locally, is important to avoid inflation which may happen when there is an injection of cash to the poorest without any increase in the overall level of the products and services available which are being or will be purchased.

These actions if properly executed should lead to more money circulating into the country's (or world's) wealth and have helped alleviate the poverty of the poorest in the process.

Note that it is not the extra circulation that is important per se, but the extra transactions made possible because people have extra money to do the transactions that they want to do, which they otherwise would not be able to do.

There should be some element of increased tax take for the government from the additional transactions and profits arising from them, which should help towards servicing the extra debt.

The process would need repeating, on a regular basis, to keep the poorest, and so all the potential consumers, spending and fuelling the economy's growth and wealth creation for all.

In a very gentle small scale way the UK's tax credit and pension credit system has been benefiting the UK economy and by its small scale addition to the nation's spending power has boosted the UK economy and alleviated poverty to a small extent and has avoided adding too much to inflation in the UK. In mid 2006 the exchange markets did react adversely to the news that the UK government was borrowing a little more but over the course of that year the strength of the economy saw a much improved exchange rate performance.

The UK already provides evidence that the basic bolstering of spending power of the poorer parts of society is beneficial to the economy.

What is needed is a realisation that a much, much larger increase is possible and desirable.

Realistically one cannot expect that we will persuade anyone to do the borrowing for all the annual spending power of the nation all in one year to produce the enormous increase in economic growth that could be done, and a smaller scale start would be a more realistic aim.

The vaccination program finance plan - to borrow now and finance it and pay for it out of the next ten years' aid budgets - shows the same basic features of the above loan plan; spending can happen now to do some good and to change and save lives now, whilst the payment is met out of the country's and world's future income. The spending actually boosts the industries involved in that the vaccine producers and medical staff to deliver the injections are all paid for now, so boosting the world economy now. Obviously there is a time to pay later for this on the vaccination program finance plan loan repayments.

Clearly each country must look to secure its increase in food production or supplies for its population to counter the food price inflation issues noted previously, however I hope I have explained how any country could try to adopt these economic plans and policies in order to boost its poor, its economy and all its citizens' wealth and prospects and life chances.

THE NEED FOR APPROPRIATE INTERVENTION

CHAPTER EIGHTEEN

WHY WE SHOULD TAKE ACTION TO STOP POVERTY AROUND THE WORLD

My point is, this boost to the poor and the poorest is for everyone's economic benefit - it should be done not only to alleviate the unnecessary suffering of those in poverty (reason enough, of course), but also because everyone should gain from the increased economic activity levels, when the systems around the world are ensuring those that might suffer are in fact being used to inject money into the economic system and by being consumers with spending power so provided they are acting as the source of wealth flowing up from them to all in the system.

Everyone on the planet can gain here.

Where is the profit from those who can't buy your products? Don't all businesses want more customers and turnover?

How much money would there be if all the continents could grow as the American economy has since it filled up USA (i.e. by economic and industrial growth alone without gains by conquest). Answer me this - did the American economy do better or worse from the arrival of the tiger economies or China on the scene? Are companies selling more to and profiting more from those countries now they have consumers who are wealthier than they were before or not? Would the world economy be worse or better, if all their citizens had money to spend on their needs and wants?

The successful pre-established companies and countries will always be well placed to do brilliantly and grow even richer - they need to invest in some potential customers.

However, perhaps, that can only be done by government(s) initially - there will be a payback for all.

China and India are joining the consumer world - why not work to get Africa, the Middle East and South America, in fact, all the world, and indeed all the poor citizens in every country, there too.

Ending poverty is not just for the poor; who knows how much we will all benefit in non financial dimensions by an enriched life free from unnecessary pain, anger, horror and guilt.

Don't you wish your lives had not witnessed and not experienced all of those emotions, sometimes on a relentless, unchanging basis from some of the horrors inflicted upon many in our world?

I know I could have lived better without these horrors in our world.

How much will we all gain and enjoy from the creativity of those in those countries freed to show their talents?

No one should be excluded, or we diminish all of us from what we could be, or could achieve.

THE NEED FOR APPROPRIATE INTERVENTION

CHAPTER NINETEEN
POLITICAL REASSURANCE AND
THE ROLE OF GOVERNMENTS IN ECONOMICS

I am not party political - even if I have had a long interest in watching and some knowledge of politics.

I believe free trade capitalism is the right path for the world, but with the sort of social security to alleviate hardship and poverty that has served the United Kingdom so well. Is there a British political party that doesn't espouse that now? There are only differences over extent, organisation, method and delivery.

I do believe however that when the market fails to deliver, governments should be stepping in to ensure that there is a correction to the systems to ensure sensible things can happen to overcome the shortcomings of the market's operation and any distortion due to perhaps inappropriate human selfishness, such as criminal misappropriation, or non-delivery of bargained for goods or services, or due to inherent mathematical side effects of the economic system.

Clearly there are similar aspects where market operations or considerations distort sensible approaches to preventing pollution etc, or lead to dysfunctional decisions, or dysfunctional distorted science or medical research for commercial gain and profit rather than best human outcome; e.g. producing endless treatments to generate indefinite income rather than outright cures, for which there is no profit motive, just moral imperative.

Whilst laws and good regulation of industries or alternatively individual, or corporate, ethical behaviour may address some of these issues, in respect of the economics and mathematics of money, it will only be co-operative action by our governments and leaders that will be able to overcome the shortcomings of money and to make the economic arrangements necessary to achieve this.

Obviously trade barriers between countries are an issue that gets in the way of co-operation - in a way they merely distort a price mechanism. That is why the losers on price complain it is down to the barriers and obviously that is true and it propels the extremes that capitalism naturally generates to be more exaggerated. Clearly those gaining from higher prices will not want to give them up unless there is some trade off or deal. The international negotiations could just be viewed as an extension of market negotiations of the terms of market pricing, albeit that may be little comfort to those seeking to negotiate changes.

THE NEED FOR APPROPRIATE INTERVENTION

CHAPTER TWENTY

THE NEED TO IMPROVE OUR CAPITALISM

Those people at the bottom of each country and those countries at the bottom suffer, perhaps more than they need. Capitalism needs some mechanism to ensure its security and rectify its shortcomings. It is a brilliant system for delivering what we want and for those that make it, and for most of the rest it is ok and they can live in hope of the dream, but for those at the bottom particularly those whose countries are at the bottom there is not enough hope.

Capitalism doesn't deliver for their wants and needs.

As it stands, it never can.

We can change all that now –

to rectify and transform the plight of those at the bottom and use this act to drive forward every economy at all levels towards much more economic activity and growth and opportunity.

There are dangers of too quick a growth, if we are not aware and ready to prevent these downsides. However if we can understand properly what we need to guard against, in overtrading and in initial transient high levels of activity followed by more steady state slightly lower activity levels in particular organisations and what that will mean for employment, inflation etc., and so forth, to allow these problems to be overcome, then the opportunities for the world to improve its economic state and performance is virtually boundless.

We just need to understand how and get the will to do it, and do it, with care, on an enormous scale, when we are ready to dare to do so.

We need to get it started somewhere first, of course.

A VERY IMPORTANT DANGER TO AVOID

CHAPTER TWENTY ONE

A FURTHER DANGER TO AVOID, BUT

A SOLUTION TO THE PROBLEM OF POVERTY

CAN BE FOUND

Our systems of money need to be changed, even if you do not like my loan from the future idea or find a problem with it that stops its use. I appreciate the loan accounting proposed may appear to some as a little bit of a cheat. This is not a mistake however, and it is not ignorance - it is just an appropriate way to do it when you understand what I am saying fully. However I realise that having the world open an almost infinite, indefinite line of credit to itself, will be too extreme for many and just "not playing the game", however useful it might actually be. The shortcut accounting outlined is easy to ridicule and dismiss, unless you understand why a deliberate break with normal accounting and with the relentless operation of money is needed to overcome this and change the mathematics.

I have some other reasons why this way of doing the loan "from the future" is better than one more conventional alternative of just raising money by loan from the banks to do this arrangement.

There is no limit to the size of the constant to be added under my proposal, i.e. we could envisage creating an unlimited line of credit to the world's economy, whereas if we must raise money conventionally from the banks we will be limited to the amount available from them. Indeed if we reach that limit, the bank, or banks and economies that depend upon them may collapse, much like Adam Smith describes some Scottish banks did collapse when they tried to expand economic and trading activity by lending freely to all or many traders in Scotland in his age.

I have a slightly different analysis and view of those situations to Adam Smith to offer the world. The overtrading collapses resulted from not enough money being available to those traders genuinely expanding their activities, and available to the banks involved, for long enough to allow the new economic projects and new businesses to deliver successful payback. Perhaps there was also an element of Enron style deception from some traders about their expansion and ever increasing debt levels drawn on borrowing from the banks to disguise their failing situations.

The consequence of the failure of the bank when it just ran out of funds from over fast expansion and the consequent lack of further finance availability was the cause of the dire economic consequences for the Scottish economy that followed, much as happens after all crashes when people are reluctant to invest in new ventures.

With more care, or better audits perhaps, and most importantly supporting finance, the bank collapses could be avoided and the genuine businesses allowed to progress to successful fruition and payback.

It is most often the restriction in finance for economic activity that restricts that activity, although there may be other limits in circumstances where finance is freely made available.

In a restricted, limited economic system of money, the mathematical operation of money transactions driving poor and rich apart may well be one driving force behind boom and bust in such economies; we may now be able to design a way to overcome this problem too. Well timed use of "loan(s) from the future" alone may do this.

Those that dismiss my loan plan as bad accounting and bad economics and put it down to a lack of understanding of how money is raised and used by the current international institutions, will have missed and not understood the implications of some of the points I have in mind and why my suggestion is appropriate. A break in the chain of the tyranny of money must be sought in any appropriate solution.

In any event, whether the loan concept is accepted or rejected, it will not change the fact that the tool of money needs to be modified for its unforgiving mathematics, and used much better by all, to produce better outcomes for the world and all people.

Of course it would be best if the international community could agree a common course of action.

My contribution is to have identified certain key aspects of the problem of poverty, wealth and money, so as to allow people, economists, governments and mathematicians the opportunity to either use my solution, or find their own.

So, for those economists and politicians who would reject my plan, ask them what they will do or are doing instead to solve the mathematics of money, and poverty for all time.

They now have an analysis of the problem, so where are their solutions?

We can solve this problem of poverty now, in our generation, and very, very quickly, if we want to, so please help make the progress, that we all need, happen, and happen in a peaceful way, sooner rather than later.

ON THE REAL CAUSES OF THE RECESSION, BANKING AND CREDIT CRISES 2007/2008

A conventional analysis of our current crises

18th November 2008

ON THE REAL CAUSES OF THE RECESSION, BANKING AND CREDIT CRISES 2007/2008

A conventional analysis of our current crises

18th November 2008

This analysis is in copyright.

Copyright © Colin Richard Webb 2008

All rights reserved. The moral rights of the author have been asserted.

This publication is in copyright. Subject only to statutory exception and to the relevant collective licensing agreements, no part of this publication may be reproduced, stored in a retrieval system, or transmitted in any form or by any means, electrical, mechanical, photocopying, recording or otherwise, without the prior permission of the copyright owner, Colin Richard Webb.

This analysis is a collection of personal views of the current crises by Colin Richard Webb, author of "The Economics of Money, Poverty and Wealth and What We Should Do About It" ISBN 978-0-9558482-0-9

CONTENTS

1. On The Real Causes of the Recession, Banking and Credit Crises 2007/2008   73-94

2. Note on timing   95

3. Minor Notes - on timing of US politics and on the Mark to Market Debate   96

4. Important Note on the Trade Cycle and the Operation of the Mathematics of Money   97

ON THE REAL CAUSES OF THE RECESSION, BANKING AND CREDIT CRISES 2007/2008

A conventional analysis of our current crises
18th November 2008

As we seek Keynesian solutions to stave off the impending recession, should we not think about whether what Keynes warned us about in his chapter 22 "Notes on The Trade Cycle" as the cause of the transition from boom to bust has taken place this time.

I believe it is the outcome and consequences of a re-assessment of a factor in what Keynes called the "marginal efficiency of capital" that has indeed been, perhaps, the main factor leading to the end of the boom and start of recession. In other words Keynes had successfully identified this aspect of the trade cycle and had written his chapter to help us avoid what has happened, but his ideas on this have fallen into disuse and we have forgotten them at our peril.

There are always many factors in a worldwide series of events such as we have seen unfolding and it is too simplistic to consider there to have been a single cause of course, but I believe my analysis is identifying some key aspects that have been involved in creating our current recession.

I hope that by identifying these aspects and making them more widely known that we can find a better set of solutions to the downturn in the months and years ahead by better understanding the factors that have produced our current difficulties.

No one should think this is a complete analysis or will describe or identify all factors that have occurred. How could any current analysis hope to do that; we are all too close to events to be able to step back and see all that has gone on. It may take economists and economic historians years or decades to really cover it all, to analyse and to understand it; there are a great many things that have been happening in the world at this time. However I hope I have identified some key factors that we should be seeking to address in finding ways to reduce this recession and move the world back to faster growth and progress.

I think you will find that one of the triggers for this change in the "marginal efficiency of capital" may have been bringing in "fair valuation" for assets valued by discounting future expected transactions as proposed and introduced by the International Accounting Standards Board("IASB"). I note in particular the introduction of the financial instruments and derivatives' International Financial Reporting Standard in the UK for periods commencing on or after 1st January 2007, has indeed required many of the affected businesses to be re-assessing and reporting (for example, for their interim 2007 half year results impact in August 2007 and for every set thereafter) their revised attitudes to risk and interest or discount rates used in valuation of their assets.

This may have been extended, or should I say compounded, later with the US Securities Exchange Commission allowing the use of IASB International Financial Reporting Standards ("IFRS") for some US company reporting from November 2007, on a voluntary adoption basis, which may have been a factor in some reporting of results during 2008 and market reactions to them.

I note the unfortunate coincidence that the first half year interim results for 2007 may well have been reporting the cost impacts on company results of the first waves of excessive energy price rises (from winter 2006 rises etc), revising expectations of profits downwards with the extra costs impacting adversely on the marginal efficiency of capital, just as the derivatives' IFRS disclosures may have been also reflecting reported changes in discount rates and interest rate risk pricing by reporting companies.

No doubt some excessive, and in some cases fraudulent, instances of excessive borrowing by individuals or of excessive lending by companies may have been present, but much and indeed the vast majority of the world's lending and borrowing will have been by ordinary honest individuals and companies and at reasonable levels given the interest rates and earnings and asset values at the time they were done.

Perhaps some of the problem has been, as Keynes might have said, not using a high enough interest rate policy in a timely manner to curtail an excess of boom near the peak (i.e. near the end) of the boom period. Whilst this might be true there has been much else happening and whether interest rates alone could have pre-empted and prevented the downturn is a moot point because we are now in one. Keynes did make it clear that once the "marginal efficiency of capital" had changed then confidence might collapse to the point no amount of practicable central bank interest rate cuts in the downturn would necessarily be capable of restoring matters to what they were. So we arrive beyond conventional monetary tools and into the realms of fiscal stimulus to encourage spending or investment to bolster the world economy. This may be all well and good, and among conventional economics' last weapons of defence against the downturn.

However our current malaise and discomfort is in part self-inflicted by creating a re-evaluation of the "marginal efficiency of capital" or the pricing of risk which is so central to such an evaluation.

This has created much of the reduction in the balance sheets of the banks and businesses and so the apparent "destruction" of the base of capital with catastrophic consequences on both the attitude to risk and leveraging providing a double whammy of lower leveraging corresponding to higher required interest/discount rates and a lower balance sheet capital base from which to lever up from. These revised levels can no longer support the previous, perhaps sensible at the time, levels of activity in the lending markets, which may have been sensible for the interest rates and risk assessments being made before the IFRS was introduced and prompted the reassessment of the interest/discount rates and pricing of risk which has spread across the world's markets and investors and so triggered the end of boom and start of recession.

The solution to these credit crunch factors will require not just the restoration of balance sheet capital but also a return to the previous assessments of the appropriate pricing of risk and the marginal efficiency of capital in order to allow the leveraging to return to those 2007 levels which will allow lending and credit availability to return to those levels. No one and particularly not the banks can restore that level of lending and credit availability without a return to those levels of marginal efficiency of capital.

In contrast to this necessary step to recovery (preferably sooner, but eventually later anyway), we are instead currently going through a consolidation of the views that say what we used before as the price of risk and the marginal efficiency of capital was wrong and too low and what we currently have and are using is better. The consequence of this mistaken approach must be a loss of and destruction of leveraged up capital financing and the terrible downturn consequences of these real higher prices of capital and higher required returns and interest rates.

We need to realise that we must reverse this view and realise that it is the level we are now adopting that is too high and has caused the crunch of credit availability by reducing leveraging and we need to return to the assessments of marginal efficiency of capital and levels of risk pricing that we were using before, so that leveraging and credit availability can return.

The triple whammy on top of this collapse of capital and leveraged capital we have suffered is that products like toxic debt and subprime sliced and diced debts may have been created to allow banks and companies to pick and choose valuations for a particular parcel of assets.

The effect of these is to allow substantial amounts of good asset value to be bundled with a little bad asset value and allow one to value it anywhere in between these values depending on one's risk assessment and discounting calculations such that the impact of a bad debt write down to reflect the bad "subprime" element can be magnified out of all proportion to hide one's good asset value and write off as much as one wanted from one's profit (and so reduce tax bills).

Hence a small amount of subprime loss of capital can be magnified up to much larger amounts.

Of course if you want to explain these enormous losses and convince everyone the subprime losses were the real cause for it all, some might need to generate large amounts of actual subprime losses by collapsing the housing market prices. This has perhaps occurred with consequent write down effect for the toxic debts. However the change in the "marginal efficiency of capital" or everyone's expectation of pricing risk and the change in required returns this implies would lead to a fall in all asset values, be they properties or shares etc.

The scope for fraud when different values could be chosen depending upon one's views of the pricing of risk and the future course of events has been immense.

Please note that this would be so whether any subprime debt had actually failed or not and so will remain an issue into the future whether subprime and toxic debt assets are bought up or not.

Of course actual failures and outright frauds using subprime debts make the situation far worse, but were also convenient for many seeking a devaluation of assets (perhaps so they could be sold on or extracted for a song).

Of course talk of doom and gloom also suited some to allow them to proceed to revaluation downwards for their assets, with write offs against profits and for tax reduction purposes.

Of course bail out money availability, whether raised by rights issues or government or third party injection of capital, might just encourage one to pretend things were worse than they were so one could get access to the extra cash.

Of course no one would want to trade a valuable but lowly valued asset for that low value unless it was to their friends etc. and this may be one reason take up of government money available to buy toxic debt may have been disappointing to governments seeking to solve the crisis that way.

Of course when one can effectively bet on a company's failure and swap its real value away to leave behind a failing shell then one can collect its real value when the lowly valued assets one swapped bring in its real value, not to the original company, but to you and your future profits later and one can also collect on one's bet it will fail and collect twice over. Does that sound familiar? Or have we just seen only a failed company with inexplicable collapse and the collection of the money bet on the company failing so far? These activities look like fraud but what transactions have occurred – a swap of assets at the values the IASB fair valuation basis would permit. One cannot say that is fraud, can you?

The scope for fraud will remain immense as long as the fair valuation discounting back future transactions basis and rules remain in use, because they require managements to forecast their organisation's future flows of money in order to discount them back to present values for their assets. As such this requires crystal ball gazing by the management to be checked by crystal ball gazing by any auditor asked to do the impossible task of verification of the values. Liability to investors is escaped and avoided because no one could say anyone could have certain knowledge of the future.

This basis completely undermines investor reassurance in reported figures, which at best depend on management's best judgment or best guess at the future, and at worst is a fraudster's paradise.

No doubt some accountants will argue that all the work involved in this fair valuation work is worthwhile and it may be for them. The IASB IFRS fair valuation discounting future transactions basis is an accountant's job creation scheme of complex calculations par excellence, but involves a cost that the rest of society cannot bear to meet.

Investors are being asked to invest in shares based upon a management forecast of the future and its audited figures audited by similar crystal ball gazing and no historic cost data. Historic cost traditionally allowed objective verification procedures rather than subjective judgments and allowed each investor to assess "actual" company performance as stated in historic cost terms in the light of their own knowledge of what may have happened in the meantime to costs and the market conditions at the moment of investment. No one can do this with valuations based on assessments of the future as no one can actually foresee the future.

The IASB fair valuation basis although perhaps laudable on some theoretical basis of seeking the current or present value at a given time and perhaps in principle capable of being no different to the pricing of assets that should be present in an investment market in fact in practice has been a disaster as should be self evident from the crises we have all been living through. The realities of people's current behaviour in business and the markets was not taken into account and considered thoroughly enough, despite all the vast amounts of time that had been spent by official bodies in arguing about the theory of fair valuation and its possible impacts.

No one seems to have asked, "Could this cause a downturn?", or, "What would its effect be on "the marginal efficiency of capital"?", or if they did, then the IASB seem to have concluded incorrectly, in my view, that fair valuation would make no difference.

I note that there are many, around the world, who have lost their jobs so far in this recession who will certainly know that there has been a difference caused to their lives.

Keynes identifies revisions to the expected efficiency of capital as, if not causal (and it might be), then certainly present early on occasion of the cessation of boom and start of bust and the crisis moments of that change. Note Keynes' marginal efficiency of capital strictly involves consideration of future returns and so expectations of future costs of production so that price shocks to food, energy, oil and commodities could each and all be said to have caused the changes to the marginal efficiency of capital.

I note again the unfortunate coincidence that the first half year interim results for 2007 may well have been reporting the cost impacts on company results of the first waves of excessive energy price rises (from winter 2006 rises etc), revising expectations of profits downwards with the extra costs impacting adversely on the marginal efficiency of capital, just as the derivatives' IFRS disclosures may have been also reflecting reported changes in discount rates and interest rate risk pricing by reporting companies.

However I note that whatever the specific causes of the August 2007 stock market falls, the stock market falls prompted and were, I think, an initial cause, amongst others, for funds to flee shares and stocks and find refuge in temporarily safer investments in these food, oil, energy and other commodities leading to much of their abrupt price increases, aggravated by any particular industry vested interest exploitation of exaggerated price increases for profit purposes.

Did any company involved in genetically modified food production buy up or increase their investments in stocks of food, so aggravating food and seed prices?

These situations were also perhaps aggravated by hedge fund operations and hedge pay-offs, where, for instance, the effect of the natural hedging pairing of dollar exchange rate and oil price movements was the most obvious manifestation of an exacerbation of the problems. Clearly it is an arena of debate as to whether hedging as an activity is a good or bad part of the markets and arbitrage system. However where funds claiming to act as vehicles for hedging turned their accumulated wealth into merely additional capital at risk and turned themselves into additional speculators and gamblers at the market casino then they distorted markets merely by where they placed their enormous bets. So in part the world economic system entered a new era of trouble and turmoil where it appeared that the hedging tail could wag the investment market dog.

Whoever invested in these stocks of commodities etc, and for whatever reason, will have pushed their prices up and increased the costs feeding into the marginal efficiency of capital evaluations.

These price shocks each feed into a change in the marginal efficiency of capital as their impact is felt throughout the economies of the world in increased costs and reduced profits in the world's businesses thus propelling us towards downturn as they each deal with their increased costs and everyone prepares themselves for the downturn with defensive and risk averse behaviour which the lower profit results provoke. Companies shed jobs to lower their costs and this leads all to fear and seek to hold onto their cash and financial resources and not spend them or risk them.

A self fulfilling reaction to the higher costs produces the downturn recession. Perhaps such worldwide processes cannot be stopped once they are in motion, however they depend on human behaviour and reactions and I believe that if people can understand the processes and what might stop it then we can all act to prevent it.

Northern Rock's rescue proved that people in the middle of a run on a bank can react immediately and change their behaviour when given the necessary information, understanding and reassurance (in that case an open ended unlimited guarantee to secure their deposits stopped the run on the bank in a day, or even just hours).

It has to be hoped that changing people's expectations and attitudes can be a two-way set of processes, even if these will not be directly reversible.

Certainly people's expectation of house prices in the US and UK have suffered from stories and ideas circulated in late 2007 about the nature of the US housing markets and UK housing market. It has to be expected that to some extent misinformation about the subprime losses were used to cover up or hide some stock market losses made by investment managers who would have found it easier to blame subprime defaulters than their own bad investment decisions for their investment company stock market losses. However there will also have been a devaluing toxic debt asset valuation agenda by some pitching comments into the debates over the crisis at the end of 2007.

Into that mix was fed two other salient academic ideas, which may have been disproportionately influential in the US housing downturn because of their media coverage. One, a report by the IMF on net asset value growth that I'll return to below, and one, a view by one professor, aired on TV News across the US, that the average price of US housing was in 2007 at an all time high and much higher than at other times in the previous hundred years such that perhaps an early twentieth century average price was a more appropriate long term pricing for housing that should be expected, which implied almost all the price rises of the last 20 to 30 years or more should be reversed.

It is almost beyond belief that a serious economist could have these views yet alone spread them to an unsuspecting public. It is self-evident that the pricing of an item in a market is its current price.

No one expects to use the prices of 20 or 30, or up to 80 years ago – the notion is absurd – no one goes to the shops and expects they can say to the shopkeeper "this product I want to buy was cheaper 20 to 30 years ago so that is the price I should be charged" and yet that is what the US people were being asked to accept when it came to views on house pricing. They were unreasonably invited to think that all their house prices had been excessive over the previous years and surprisingly agreed this proposition and caused their housing market values to collapse with resultant creation and aggravation of the subprime actual defaults and toxic asset write downs.

The late 2007 report by the IMF that noted housing net asset values over an extended long period had significantly outstripped the growth of other assets further suggested in the view of the IMF economists reporting this finding that house pricing was overstated by up to some 40%. However this report's conclusions may have been mistaken.

This is not to say some house pricing may not have been a little excessive but it is to say most of the extra asset growth should have been expected to be that way.

It was possible to look at the net asset growth of housing and other assets another way. After adjusting for inflation effects one could arrive at the net asset growth of house values, or its return on initial capital, as being approximately 3 to 4 times that of the other assets.

The report's findings of greater growth in housing asset values compared to other investment asset growth should not have been a surprise, although it was treated as one and presented by some as evidence of a housing bubble that needed to burst.

The reason that housing should outstrip other asset growth is that house prices depend upon the loans that earnings can support and earnings can support a multiple of that level of earnings as a level of loan, as the loan can stretch over many years as a long term commitment. The appropriate level of earnings will depend on investment decisions made by companies about employing people based upon their required rate of return and investment plans and so earnings level will correspond to that level of required rate of return of investment. Surely then it is obvious that the house prices will quite reasonably depend on a multiple of that earning level and so produce a rate of growth and return that is a multiple of those earning levels and as such the rate of return of the growth in housing value should be a multiple above the rate of asset growth of other investments invested in on the basis of the normal required rate of return.

As a result of an apparent lack of understanding of this by the IMF and a drive to burst the claimed "housing bubble" we have entered a severe collapse of the housing markets in both US and UK that has self-actualised the existence of the "housing bubble" by creating house price falls, aggravated the subprime crisis, created some of the credit crunch, produced actual negative equity, actual defaults and repossessions and hence accelerated us all into recession out of housing market price reductions.

Obviously some outrageous mortgage selling practices in US were uncovered and some of the subprime losses created were due to excessive or fraudulent lending practices and excessive property pricing leading to excessive debt and subsequent defaults, some as a result of outright frauds.

However in terms of real long term values, if one can finance the acquisitions, housing may well have reached levels of incredible bargain compared to earnings, certainly in the UK (which was not subject to anything like the same extent as the US subprime to any of the extreme mortgage mis-selling practices), and if the market downturn and descent were not in full swing at the moment. Not that credit or mortgage financing is available, given the credit crunch and all the unfortunate misplaced revised attitudes of everyone to giving and taking out debt.

I want to return now to one trigger for all this which I think was the IASB IFRS and its fair value discounting back from future events basis of accounting. I think it will continue to produce and provoke problems in the assessment of the marginal efficiency of capital while it continues to be used as a basis for reporting company results and attitudes to risk, at least until everyone in the markets recognises and takes its impact into account and ignores these impacts it can cause, as far as it is possible to do so and they are able to do so.

Keynes' efficiency of capital is the expected future returns discounted back to their present value compared to the relevant current replacement costs and is in effect the discount rate in use. In Keynes' day historic cost was accounted for and provides a near approximation to the current replacement cost if there has been no great change in prices or cost in the period between the historic transaction and the current moment in which the replacement cost is being assessed. Not ideal perhaps but at least investors can obtain reasonable verifiable data and form judgments on it from their knowledge of what is happening in the markets and economies. This is preferable to what the fair valuation look into the future bases have brought and will bring us.

The IASB fair valuation attempts to usurp market determination of the replacement cost, otherwise known as current price of an investment or asset, by inserting by accounting the management's assessment of the present value of future receipts, which depends upon their assessment of the appropriate future discounting rates.

It is a mistake in principle which is producing unfortunate feedback loops, such as the pension scheme deficits from share value falls feeding back to potential company balance sheet deficits, which feed back to lower share values etc. Perhaps an engineering or systems approach to the mathematical analysis of, or perspective on, our economic systems might produce useful insights into the feedback effects involved.

However it is clear there is a vicious circle of reducing balance sheets and capital assets aggravated by company greed seeking to hide real value and reduce tax liabilities by asset value write down.

Far more serious than this, bad though that is, is the reduction of capital inherent in the fair valuation assessment (in actual practice) and its knock on effects to the capital base and financing potential of the world.

Using lower asset values and capital values does not just devastate balance sheets in companies and banks (and pension funds - lest we forget the demise of final salary schemes), but it also lowers actual levels of capital in the world.

With less capital there must be less activity in the world as capital is a key essential element of any enterprise in a capitalist system.

We face the worst crisis of capitalism we have ever seen and it has been self-inflicted on the world's financial system by accountants who have not understood the full economic effect of their accounting changes, which the IASB and Sir David Tweedie told us, and tell us, in principle, should make no difference and may, in theory, be neutral, but which many accountants and large businesses know in practice will save them taxes and allow them to pick and choose the valuations of their balance sheet assets and results, with a practical tax saving bias towards downward reporting although I note there may also be risks of false upward reporting.

The Chartered Accountant's "Accountancy" magazine illustrated the effect of using one IFRS with an example company named, "Pick and Choose plc" although repeating a mantra that it would not change the results and net assets of companies.

There is actually bound to be greater variability and volatility in the reporting of profits and losses and hence more volatile stock markets in short run reactions but also in more sweeping market responses to results and net assets reported across many companies in the same periods. There is already research evidence of such greater variability in reporting in respect of the use of fair valuation in actual pension fund reporting in the UK where fair valuation was introduced some time ago.

Why haven't more bankers, large businesses or accountants informed the government about the possibilities with the fair valuation basis? One could speculate that perhaps some expect to gain at the expense of taxpayers from its use – both from write downs reducing their profits and corporation tax and now from bailout cash injections however structured.

Perhaps some have no knowledge or understanding of the devastating economic effect their change has brought to us all, or perhaps some just don't care as long as they are making their bundle and are seeing themselves alright.

When some might know some are, or could be, up to valuation tricks or sharp practice no wonder some bankers cannot trust each other's figures or each other enough to lend to one another, and government and regulators plead for more transparency.

Unfortunately one could also speculate that some bankers may be also playing at increasing their wholesale market price to increase their retail pricing of loans and credit and in this they have taken a leaf out of the energy industries, gas and electric companies, and oil and petrol industry company playbooks on how to justify high retail pricing with high wholesale market prices, or promised "essential" future long term investment in order to make excessive short term profits and in reality to create high management rewards, high dividends and high share price for their short term gain.

Governments need to find a way regulators can overcome these possibly present wholesale pricing cartel-like arrangements or herd basis effects whether it is in oil, gas, electricity or banking.

Otherwise normal previous levels of pricing will not return. Also random price shocks could be inflicted by an industry upon our economies and produce a change in the marginal efficiency of capital and so trigger downturn.

Indeed there may be a case for the energy companies to answer here as their price increases in recent years may well have been in part causal to the creation of this downturn. Indeed they may need to be called upon or required to reverse all these rises in prices of recent years to help rescue the world economy at this time of its dire need; a need which personal greed for profit, pay and company share/share option price gains may have fuelled far more than any individual borrower has done.

Further although the speculative impact on pricing of oil and food may have now evaporated and these costs have fallen back, energy costs have not fallen back as quickly as they could have and this will prolong the cost shock of these costs and slow the recovery of the economy unless this is changed.

However the more lasting effect of the price shocks has been to alter the perception of the marginal efficiency of capital, asset price levels and appropriate leveraging and attitudes to debt levels and credit. We will not recover the credit levels until we reverse that attitude to the revised marginal efficiency of capital and cost of capital or pricing of risk and return to the before loss of boom levels.

Of course Keynes warned us that after the crisis point and the change in efficiency of capital moves the world from boom to bust, next will come increased real interest rates. Now we can see this may be because of the collapse of the supply of credit and investment capital availability because of, in effect, the revised increased pricing of risk and corresponding reduced level of leveraging appropriate to that revised expected or required rate of return. The increased required rates of return for investment represent or reflect that reluctance to risk making investments and to seek the safety of liquid assets that characterize the post-crisis period and also, with fear of an impending reduction in sales, prompt the shedding of employees and costs to prepare businesses for lower expected activity and cash flow levels.

Distinguishing between downturn uplift in interest rates, perhaps rigged wholesale interest rates and the terrible consequences for interest rates of the credit crunch from loss of leveraging and loss of capital and downturn for credit availability will be very difficult. We need to find a solution for the latter before we can address the other aspects.

It is ironic that the intent of fair valuation may have been to prevent companies getting carried away with their reported historic cost profits, paying out too much and denuding their balance sheets of needed capital so not safeguarding themselves against future failure, but the unfortunate effect of "protective" accounting fair valuation has been to cause the failure of so many companies and to jeopardize so many companies and jobs and indeed the entire world banking and financial systems.

I am not exaggerating this latter point, the use of fair valuation accounting will lead to reduced capital levels <u>and</u> reduced growth of capital with dire, short, middle and long term effects of that slower accumulation of capital for the world's economy. It will hold back human development and progress in the world as indeed it may already have done with the current onset of downturn.

Furthermore every adverse shift in the price of risk reported could trigger even more recession or downward shift in confidence leading to further recessions.

One point is that the discounting back of the future basis for IASB fair valuations may lock everyone into statements of future doom and gloom, perhaps because some do not want to reduce their asset impairment write downs and declare higher profits, but actually in any event, statements have to be made about outlook. These statements may be positive or negative, but every negative statement whether true or not may trigger market wide adverse assessment of the marginal efficiency of capital and a downturn, much as any statement of US or UK housing downward outlook runs a risk of being a self-fulfilling prophesy, like the last year.

The UK CBI gloomy unemployment forecast for 2009 may have similar unfortunate self-fulfilling effects unless more realistic assessments prevail upon everyone's mindsets.

We could do worse than going back to the previous historic cost accounting and abandoning the use of fair valuation by discounting back to present values from future estimates altogether, although this in itself can never undo all the damage already done and unfortunately still in the process of unfolding.

We must stop using the guess the future basis of evaluating fair valuation which is the current IASB basis, and definitely not spread its use, which can only lead to more uncertainty and more fraud by greedy and selfish individuals and company directors.

Obviously in the global financial markets the world needs a World Accounting Standards Body created with proper legal authority, responsibility and independence, preferably freed from the dangers of undue political or any risks of undue financial influence by any private individuals or companies or group of companies or indeed countries.

However whether this emerges out of the IASB, or replaces it, it is clear that we need a body that includes sufficient knowledge of and wisdom in Economics, as well as practical accountancy, to better understand the full economic and practical impact of the introduced standards of accounting.

We need to create World Accounting Standards, but not using the guess the future and discount back to present value fair valuations, i.e. perhaps World Accounting Standards based on an historic cost basis would be better.

Of course if we just proceed with using fair valuation based on future events and arbitrary discount rates we will face further capital destruction on balance sheets, and not just on financial services balance sheets, and further closures of activity from lack of finance and capital.

Eventually the world economy will adapt to all the uncertainty but it may take many years before the world's economy will ever earn back through future profits growth, all the lost capital and capital financing which has been lost by accounting write off of balance sheet asset value and the resultant demise of the leveraged up finance levels, that may be gone until there is restoration of capital or balance sheet values of the banks and companies etc.

It is the loss of the supply of the credit based on that leveraging up of finance above the capital base that is the credit crunch.

Until balance sheet values of capital and the marginal efficiency of capital and corresponding pricing of risk are restored the loss of possibility of credit provision is real and perhaps permanent. However the leveraging up can only restore previous capital financing levels if the marginal efficiency of capital and pricing of risk returns to the before end of boom period levels, that people are currently making the mistake of shunning and denouncing instead.

Almost last, but certainly not least, in this analysis I note that debt levels taken on to acquire assets naturally match up with the asset values of those assets on purchase, such that ideas that all our "debt fuelled" growth was bad are simply wrong. With completely genuine sensible growth you would have asset values with debt levels appropriate to them and when a re-assessment of the price of interest and risk occurs to devalue the assets it will always leave the debt levels outstanding and higher than the revised down asset values.

It does not mean any of the original growth, lending and borrowing was reckless, but just that the price of risk has been re-assessed (in this case perhaps caused recklessly as no official body appears to have anticipated that the accounting changes were going to help cause all this – Keynes would have known). Having said that we clearly have seen some reckless and excessive borrowing and lending and some fraudulent activities re sub-prime and its consequences have been evident.

It is also important to note that during the boom period, lowering interest rates as a matter of policy in order to maintain asset values in shares and properties in the US (the Greenspan method) could not be used indefinitely to stave off a halt or reduction in growth in the US economy useful though it may have been for the US economy for many years. A point had to be reached where further cuts could not in themselves sustain the economy's level of activity, i.e., organic growth from an underlying strength of economic activity is needed to support real asset value growth and the use of interest rate policy alone, useful though it may be in the short run, had to reach a limit beyond which it could not be effective.

Before that point was reached a different interest rate policy was needed and indeed a gentle rise in interest rates at the right time was needed to rein in asset value growth gently (as Keynes suggests or implies) and to allow real underlying economic activity to catch up and properly support or justify the asset value levels reached.

It was being widely acknowledged in mid 2007 before the stock market falls in August 2007 that central bank interest rate policies had remained too loose for a little too long in 2007. This recognition may have been a factor in the August 2007 stock market falls. Clearly a slightly different higher interest rate policy was needed at an earlier point in order to prevent us reaching the point of stock market falls/crash and end of boom.

Keynes warns us the recessions we could expect after the crisis point brings a boom to an end could last typically 3 to 5 years, but we have never seen such enormous loss and destruction of financial capital and leveraged finance and loss of credit availability arising from the change in marginal efficiency of capital, so it may be far worse unless we can find an alternative solution to providing capital and financing to companies.

Countries borrowing to support them from the capital markets may have a problem in that the capital is not there as it was before.

We face a conventional economic catastrophic disaster, some of which is still to fully arrive.

On a Keynesian basis we must restore the expectations of the marginal efficiency of capital before recovery will occur, although this may be difficult to achieve after such huge losses of capital and loss of leveraged capital financing, which may be a larger multiple of that capital loss and so the more significant loss.

Restoring the marginal efficiency of capital and so required rates of return and the acceptability of leveraging at previous high levels is necessary in order to recover the former capital and financing position.

So we perhaps could try an unconventional radical solution; no one has tried this before, I think.

One might be able to attempt to explain the problem and seek to persuade the world to change its current attitudes to risk pricing, investment, asset price levels (shares and properties) and spending so allowing a return to the levels before the loss of boom.

Quite a big ask and hard to achieve obviously, but perhaps worth the attempt to minimise the downturn which perhaps we cannot now stop in its tracks.

The above attempt might fail (and is most likely to be an incomplete restoration of the previous position in the short run) and so some shortfall of leveraged financing and shortfall of capital is likely to persist and create downturn unless a means of restoring the capital and leveraged financing shortfall can be found.

With this in mind I note that the radical unconventional solution to poverty proposed in my book "The Economics of Money, Poverty and Wealth and What We Should Do About It" would also allow a means of creating a line of credit and capital to banks and businesses, even though the book was written to solve a very different, and actually much bigger, problem.

In fact my suggestion would produce a means of introducing capital into the world that could produce not just a halt to the recession but start up a sustainable substantial boom, but we mustn't run before we can walk.

Colin Richard Webb

Note re timing

Of further note will be the interaction of all the short term reactions and attempted solutions to the various crises that have been attempted during the periods since the August 2007 stock market falls and the current crises of September, October and November 2008. In particular I note that the effect of various government temporary 3 month or 6 month market liquidity solutions as they came to an end may have fed adversely into markets (just as their introduction was intended to assist the markets) and their expected or actual expiration may have influenced the markets just as further rounds of quarterly reporting of results and write downs also impacted on the stock markets.

On this aspect of timing I also note it is the quarterly impact of reporting of the effect on profits of actual cost and price rises that have occurred for businesses that is the information transmission mechanism whereby actual cost increases have their effect on profit performance and indicates the actual cost increase and profit reduction effect to the markets, a little later than the price rises themselves. Hence price shocks from speculation etc in the second quarter may impact again on the stock markets with third quarter reported results and profit warnings and this is part of what we have seen in the last couple of months.

I note that the Interbank interest rate spreads jumped to much higher levels abruptly in August 2007 and remained high with high volatility thereafter, perhaps with quarterly peaks until the extreme rise in the banking "meltdown" crisis and events of the last 3 hectic months. The abrupt jump in August 2007 is clearly important in the development of the crises, however whether this was the consequence of or in part the cause of the August 2007 stock market falls or whether both were the result of some third causal factor is the key area future economic researchers will need to examine and establish. I further note that the full effects of initial oil price rises in mid 2006 may have been feeding into late 2006 energy price rises and into cost and profit result data reported by companies in the 2007 first half results etc.

Note Clearly there will have been other factors and a myriad of specific events that have happened in the last 2 years which will each have fed into and interacted with the causes I have set out in this account.

Not least of these will have been the protracted uncertainty resulting from the periods of US Presidential Candidacy and Presidential Election campaigning and the last months and days of the Republican hopes to retain power in US, as well as the global political uncertainty arising out of the Georgian war and deterioration in relations between Russia and the US.

Minor Side Note on IASB IFRS Changing just the "Mark to market" rules to the other 6 month or 12 month bases proposed in public debate so far would only widen the scope for manipulation of figures. The debate over "Mark to market" misses the big points that need to be debated: these "Mark to market" side issues are like a "straw man" to be knocked down to get people to accept the fair valuation basis of the IASB IFRS as ok, when as I have attempted to explain that in my view that in the form in which it has been currently introduced it is very definitely not ok.

Important Note on the Trade Cycle and the Operation of the Mathematics of Money

The analysis in "The Economics of Money, Poverty and Wealth and What We Should Do About It" concludes with a note that the operation of money separating itself through the mathematics of transactions alone into accumulations in the hands of the wealthy may be a causal factor behind the boom and bust of the trade cycle.

On this basis there has to be some means of getting money back around the system so it can be used by the non-wealthy to spend and maintain activity in the economy.

Where this is not achieved through the tax and benefit systems, the accumulations will inevitably eventually produce the crisis of a boom of too much money in the hands of a few who therefore chase further investment opportunities.

In contrast a shortage of money held by people lower down the system cannot sustain their spending and so fails to sustain the turnover and profitability of businesses providing those investment possibilities for the rich.

This leads to a bust as the trading returns cannot support the value of those levels of money available to invest, or maintain that value of the money available for investment. That is, the high level of money in rich hands will push prices of investments and assets up, but the underlying profits are based on the amount of money that can be spent lower down the system; sooner or later under the conventional economics of money the mismatch leads to a correction.

"The Economics of Money, Poverty and Wealth
and What We Should Do About It"

Email to Professor Sachs, at Columbia Earth Institute
Sent to se2179@columbia.edu on 25th September 2008

Please can you let Professor Sachs know about my book which may help him resolve some funding issues if he can find a way to use the ideas contained within it.

The Economics of Money, Poverty and Wealth and What We Should Do About It
by Colin Richard Webb - ISBN 978-0-9558482-0-9

I am not a Professor, but have been a Chartered Accountant and Auditor of nearly twenty years practical experience in a previous time in my life. The book is written in a fairly basic manner because I am not a very good author, however it is short and to the point and I believe it contains a gem of an idea which may be of great use to Professor Sachs and his work.

I will send a copy to the Earth Institute in the post for Professor Sachs attention, however if he or you would like to obtain a copy directly before this it can be purchased from Amazon or a number of other online stores, or an Ebook can be purchased more cheaply and more importantly without any delay from my very basic website whose only function is to allow access to my ebooks.(please do not be put off - the book is better than the website)

http://myweb.tiscali.co.uk/wholenewwebbworld/

Although my book suggests a "loan from the future" - it is a "loan" that does not need repayment - it is really a suggestion that we inject money into the economic systems not by lending to the banks but by lending to the poorest - ensuring money gets where it is needed throughout the system - not just to the banks but to everyone (who can of course always put their money into their banks and into the banks with their deposits so resolving the credit crunch a slightly different and better way.) For those who do not have bank accounts yet - perhaps the accounts could be opened for them and their money deposited for them in anticipation of its use as they wish when they are given access to them. Central banks can thus issue money into the bank sector whilst also preparing the way for access to money for the poorest which they can decide how to spend later.

With my best wishes for Professor Sachs and his good work,

Colin Richard Webb

Post Script Explanatory Note (Not part of Email sent)

"Lending to the poorest" is an unfortunate phrase – one could think that was what the subprime lenders had been doing – and yet their motives seem to have been merely their own selfish gain at the expense of the poor so badly used by them and at the expense of investors so badly misled by the subprime lenders, creators and marketeers.

However in my framework and sense the phrase means giving the poorest their money out of the "loan from the future" so that they, and all, can spend that money and so stoke up economic activity on a much, much greater scale than the world has ever seen and to avoid the consequences of poverty otherwise present in the world; the "loan from the future" is not intended to be repaid, but to be a completely different way for the world to use the tool of money in order to rectify and overcome its inherent mathematical flaws that otherwise create poverty.

"An original idea to alleviate poverty"

Email to United Nations

Sent to haji@un.org on 17th October 2008,

International Poverty Eradication Day

I wanted to bring to your attention my book "The Economics of Money, Poverty and Wealth and What We Should Do About It" ISBN 978-0-9558482-0-9.

The book contains an original analysis and a mathematical concept involving a paradigm shift in the approach to human economics and the use of money to solve poverty around the world; I believe it contains a unique idea that could transform the planet's economics and end poverty much more quickly than current alternatives.

I would like to send a complimentary copy to Ban Ki Moon and the United Nations, and perhaps a copy for the UN library, but where should I send this to ensure someone actually reads the book, gets the idea and more importantly has a chance of using it or spreading it to others so they can decide whether to use it in one country, or around the world, to end poverty in their country or around the world.

The idea might help with the global financial crisis as well, but the book was created to address the much bigger problem of poverty that afflicts the world.

Please let me know where I can send the copies of my book so Ban Ki Moon or United Nations people can read and understand my book.

Although not elaborated in the book a key concept alluded to only in passing is that by expanding thinking on the quantity theory of money, where prices are determined by the amount of money and the level of activity, one can realise that for more activity at the same prices we must actually have more money.

With much more money created (printed if need be) and deployed sensibly we can create much more activity and by deploying the money to increase supplying activity one can limit the inflation that the conventional quantity theory of money would expect and so allow more money to create more activity thus getting increased activity and distribution of money across a larger population of the world.

The thinking in the book was created and intended to find ways we could overcome poverty and expand human activities in a faster way than the present systems allow and was about creating a boom or a super-boom for the world, but I am sure it can be easily adapted to prevent the worst of the world recession and potential for depression that the current economic systems have been producing lately.

The main original idea in the book involves a far more profound change to the world's approach to money and economics than just this.

Please help - I may have had an amazing idea, but I am quite hopeless at working out how to bring it to people's attention and get the ideas known and thought about around the world.

Colin Richard Webb

PS My book is available through Amazon and several online bookstores or an ebook can be purchased from my website at http://myweb.tiscali.co.uk/wholenewwebbworld if you don't want to wait for copies to be sent to you. Some of the book can be seen on Google Book Search, although at the moment not the central key original ideas which are later on in the book.

Post Script Explanatory Note (Not part of Email sent)

The quantity theory of money and indeed much of economic theory has a root in a position taken by the philosopher and economic theorist David Hume that for a given amount of resource at a given price adding more money would just lead to a greater price for the resource.

On a summation of all resources therefore it would be easy to conclude that adding more money to the world would only lead to higher prices; this is the view of all conventional economics, and it is wrong.

The error arises from the assumptions made, some of which are explicit but some of which are hidden in the thinking adopted. The explicit assumption in error is that the amount of the resource or each resource is fixed or constant.

The implicit error is the current totality assumption that by summating all there currently is one has included all that there could ever be.

In some varieties of this, like Ricardo, there is also an overstatement of the summation position – arising from claiming to cover all the world contains and all its resources, when one should really address all the current economy has or permits, and then realise this is in fact less than all the world contains or could contain and so one can conceive of the current world economy expanding to contain more than it currently does.

Hume's position might be valid if the resource amount was constant, or had reached its maximum limit or amount, and clearly it might be a factor of some importance where there is some delay or slowness in changing the amount of the resource involved.

However there will often be situations where this underlying assumption of a given amount of resource is not a correct assumption. In the real world more often than not there is not really a fixed limited amount of a resource and the level available that has been reached is determined more by the economic considerations of money of our current limited systems and previous assumptions than any physical or other limits.

In these situations (and there are many) where the amount of the resource can vary (specifically be increased) then the effect of adding more money will not just be adding to prices, but will be, or may be, to increase the total level of resource in use or available in the economic system. Hence if the new additional money is fully taken up by and put into use in the financial requirements of the additional activity created then it would not be available to increase the prices of other resources or activity at all. Obviously in practice perfect take up in this way would not be possible to achieve and some limited inflation of the pricing of other resources could arise unless their supply level was also expanded appropriately where possible to do so. However much depends on the specific deployment of the money and into whose hands and for what purposes the money is to be used and is actually used.

Despite this there is much in our current economic arrangements and level of delivery of goods and services to all of the world's population that could be vastly improved by making use of these ideas.

Shocking though it might be for some to realise, Hume's position, which lies at the root of the logic of conventional economics, has an incorrect assumption at its heart leading to an incorrect conclusion which is at the base of conventional economics theory re allocation of resources, pricing and the effect of the quantity of money.

I would note that if, after realizing this error, it is easy to envisage adding more money to the economic systems, it may be a little harder to take away an excess, except through inflation or money's devaluation, so some caution is still needed in the amount added.

However much is currently needed to be added to make up for the enormous shortfall in the amount of money available to most of the world's population.

We can make better use of money once we realise how to deploy and use it as a tool for all of us to improve the world and what can be done.

www.ingramcontent.com/pod-product-compliance
Ingram Content Group UK Ltd.
Pitfield, Milton Keynes, MK11 3LW, UK
UKHW041436180426
11947UKWH00007B/470